How do they work?

Puppets

Wendy Sadler

Heinemann LIBRARY

Young Explorer

www.heinemann.co.uk/library
Visit our website to find out more information about **Heinemann Library** books.

To order:
 Phone 44 (0) 1865 888066
Send a fax to 44 (0) 1865 314091
 Visit the Heinemann Bookshop at www.heinemann.co.uk/library to browse our catalogue and order online.

First published in Great Britain by Heinemann Library, Halley Court, Jordan Hill, Oxford OX2 8EJ, part of Harcourt Education.
Heinemann is a registered trademark of Harcourt Education Ltd.

Editorial: Andrew Farrow and Dan Nunn
Design: Ron Kamen and Dave Oakley/ Arnos Design
Picture Research: Hannah Taylor
Production: Duncan Gilbert
Originated by Ambassador Litho Ltd
Printed and bound in China by South China Printing Company.

The paper used to print this book comes from sustainable resources.

0 431 04966 1
09 08 07 06 05
10 9 8 7 6 5 4 3 2 1

British Library Cataloguing in Publication Data

Sadler, Wendy
  Puppets. – (How do they work?)
  1. Puppet making – Juvenile literature
  I. Title
  688.7'224

A full catalogue record for this book is available from the British Library.

Acknowledgements
The publishers would like to thank the following for permission to reproduce photographs:
Alamy Images pp. 18 (Mike Blenkinsop), **26** (Dave Pattison); Corbis pp. **5** (Julio Donoso), **14** (Jose Luis Pelaez Inc.), **15** (Werner Forman), **19** (Mitchell Gerber), **21** (Jim Sugar), **27** (John R. Jones/Papilio); Harcourt Education Ltd (Tudor Photography) pp. **4**, **6**, **7**, **8**, **9**, **10**, **11**, **12**, **13**, **17**, **22**, **23**, **28–29**; Pete Jones (ArenaPAL) p. **25**; Reuters (Jason Reed) p. **16**; Getty Images (Photodisc) p. **24**; Science Photo Library p. **20**.

Cover photograph reproduced with permission of Harcourt Education Ltd (Tudor Photography).

Every effort has been made to contact copyright holders of any material reproduced in this book. Any omissions will be rectified in subsequent printings if notice is given to the publishers.

Contents

Some words are shown in bold, **like this**. You can find out what they mean by looking in the glossary.

 Find out more about puppets at www.heinemannexplore.co.uk

Puppets

A puppet is a **model** of a person or an animal. You can move puppets using your fingers, hands, strings, or **rods**.

Puppets come in lots of different shapes and sizes. You can make your own puppets at home. You can also see puppets on television!

Finger puppets

A finger puppet is a small puppet that fits on your finger. You move the puppet by bending or moving your finger. You can even have five puppets on one hand!

your fingers go in here

Finger puppets can be made of **fabric** or **plastic**. In some finger puppets, your fingers become legs!

Hand puppets

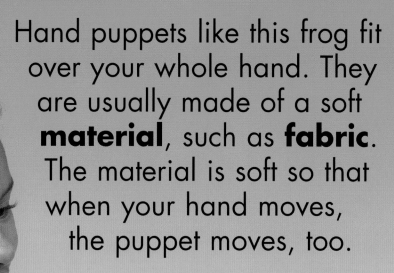

Hand puppets like this frog fit over your whole hand. They are usually made of a soft **material**, such as **fabric**. The material is soft so that when your hand moves, the puppet moves, too.

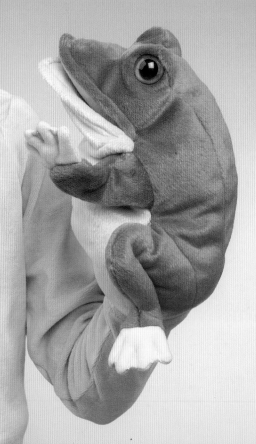

your fingers go in here

your thumb goes in here

You can make a hand puppet from a sock. Your thumb becomes the mouth of the puppet. Your fingers become the head. You can make the puppet "talk" by moving your fingers and thumb.

Puppets with legs

In some hand puppets your fingers become the legs. This puppet is a big insect. Your front two fingers become the insect's legs.

your fingers go in here

In this puppet all your fingers are used
as legs. A spider has eight legs, but you ·
have only four fingers and a thumb.
Some of the puppet legs will not have
a finger in them.

Puppets with strings

You can make
this puppet move
without even
touching it!
You move it
by pulling on
the strings.

When you pull a string tied to a leg, you lift the leg. You can make a string puppet walk by pulling the strings in the right order.

13

Puppets on rods

rods

Some puppets can be moved using **rods**. You push the rods to make different parts of the puppet move.

joints

rod

This rod puppet has **joints**. The joints let the arms move. Puppets with joints can be made to move, like real people and animals.

15

Puppet materials

Different puppets are made of different **materials**. Puppets on **rods** need to be **stiff** so they can stand up. If they were made of soft material they would just fall over!

strings

Puppets on strings are often made of wood. Wood is a stiff material. These puppets need to have **joints**.

wood

joint

Big puppets

Some puppets are very big. They can be moved by a person inside the puppet. This monster puppet has a person inside. The person moves his or her arms to make the arms of the monster move.

This is Big Bird, from the television show *Sesame Street*.

Some puppets have **controls** in their head. Pushing a button or pulling a **lever** makes the eyes or face move. Big Bird's eyes work like this.

19

Animatronics

Some puppets work using machines. They are called **animatronic** puppets. This is what the inside of an animatronic puppet looks like.

Animatronic puppets can look very real. These two animatronic animal puppets were made for a television show.

animatronic puppets

Shadow puppets

Shadow puppets can be made of thick card. The card blocks a light shining on a wall. Where the light is blocked, a shadow forms that is the same shape as the card.

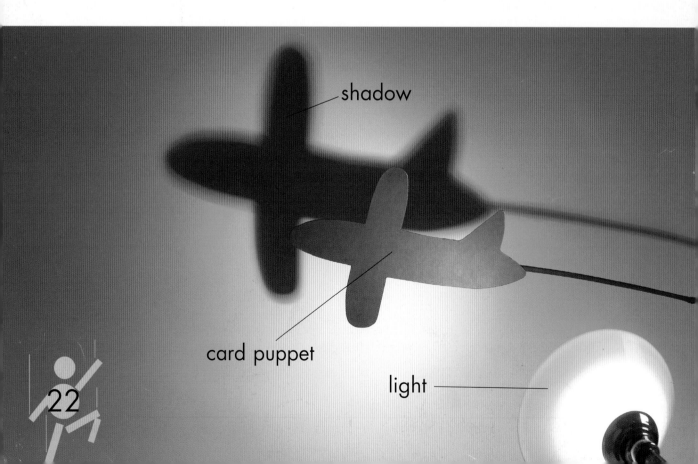

shadow

card puppet

light

You can also make shadow puppets with your hands. The shadows will get bigger if you move your hands closer to the light.

Puppets that glow in the dark

Some puppets are made of special **materials**. These make the puppets glow in the dark when a special light shines on them.

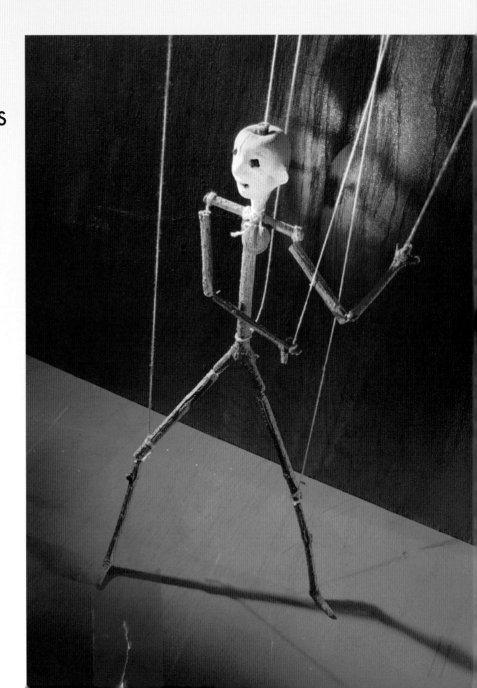

24

People who move puppets often wear black
clothes. This means they cannot be seen in
the dark. The puppets seem to be moving
by themselves, because you cannot see the
people who are moving them.

Puppet shows

These children are watching a puppet show. The puppets are moved by someone hiding inside the tall box.

String puppets need a **stage** with room above it for people to stand. This is so they can pull the strings to make the puppets move.

Put on your own puppet show

You can put on your own puppet shows by making a stage. These are some of the things you will need to do:

- Write a short story, or play, for your puppets to perform.
- Make puppets for each character in the play.
- Build a simple **stage** that can be put on a table.
- Practise your play.
- Invite people to come to see your play.

Find out more about puppets at
www.heinemannexplore.co.uk

Glossary

animatronic puppet that looks like a real animal or person. It is controlled by a machine.

controls buttons and levers that make something work

fabric soft material, such as cotton or wool

joint place where two moving things are joined together

lever simple machine that makes it easier to move something

material what something is made of

model copy of something else

plastic light material that can be made in many shapes and colours

rod long, thin pole

shadow dark shape made when something is between a surface and a bright light

stage part of a theatre where the actors or puppets perform

stiff something that is hard to bend

Find out more

More books to read

Puppet Mania! The World's Most Incredible Puppet Making Book Ever!, John Kennedy (North Light Books, 2004)

The Usborne Book of Puppets, Ken Haines, Gill Harvey and Teri Gower (Usborne Publishing Ltd, 1998)

Websites to visit

http://www.puppetuniverse.com/sock-puppet.php
Visit this website to find out how to make a sock puppet.

http://www.bbc.co.uk/cbeebies/printables/fingerpuppets/
This website will tell you how to make a finger puppet.

http://www.muppets.com
This website will tell you everything you ever wanted to know about the Muppets.

Disclaimer

All the Internet addresses (URLs) given in this book were valid at the time of going to press. However, due to the dynamic nature of the Internet, some addresses may have changed, or sites may have changed or ceased to exist since publication. While the author and Publishers regret any inconvenience this may cause readers, no responsibility for any such changes can be accepted by either the author or the Publishers.

Index

Titles in the *How Do They Work?* series include:

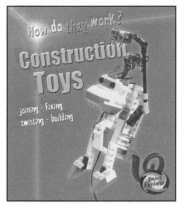

Hardback   0 431 04964 5

Hardback   0 431 04965 3

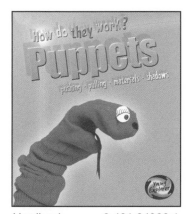

Hardback   0 431 04966 1

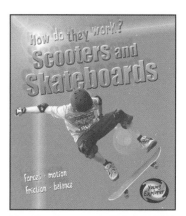

Hardback   0 431 04969 6

Hardback   0 431 04967 X

Hardback   0 431 04968 8

Find out about the other titles in this series on our website www.heinemann.co.uk/library